watercolors by **KEITH ROSE**　　　　map illustrations by **KATE RUSSELL FORBES**

EXPLORING THE LIGHTHOUSES
of North Carolina

by

CINDY COREY

THE PROVINCIAL PRESS　　　　Box 2311　　　　Chapel Hill, North Carolina 27514

Preface

Here are the lighthouses of North Carolina—those romantic sentinels on coastal sands that both welcome and warn seafarers. They stand guard where sea and land meet and appear to say: "Here America and the Tar Heel state begin."

Six of the ten lights flash from towers standing on shore, each structure identified by its own shape and marking. Two lights burn offshore from so-called "Texas" towers that rise from the sea like giant erector sets. Two lights went dark long ago but their abandoned, aged towers remain.

Several of the Tar Heel lighthouses enjoy superlative status. Cape Hatteras is America's tallest, soaring 208 feet from base to peak. Ocracoke ranks as one of the nation's oldest, dating from 1823. Oak Island is the country's newest and brightest. Constructed in 1958, it penetrates soupy weather with a 20-million candlepower intensity.

The strength of the Oak Island beacon illustrates how far lighthouses in general have advanced. Originally, open fires on seaside hills warned mariners. Then whale oil lamps served this purpose. Next came kerosene lights and finally electric lamps.

In 1823 French physicist, Augustin Fresnel, radically increased the effectiveness of lighthouses by inventing a reflector lens. The circular ridges of a Fresnel lens catch light rays from a lamp and redirect them into a single beam of extremely high intensity visible far out at sea.

Until 1789 the North Carolina Legislature authorized lighthouses; local communities built and maintained them. Following the formation of America as a nation, the Federal Government assumed that responsibility under the ninth law of the new land enacted on August 7, 1789. One of the first acts of President George Washington provided for the construction of lighthouses along coasts of the 13 original states.

The U.S. Lighthouse Service operated the beacons until 1939 when the U.S. Coast Guard absorbed the Service. Today the Coast Guard still operates the beacons and at some sites cooperates with the National Park Service in opening the seaside sentinels to visitors. At Cape Hatteras, for instance, stout-hearted visitors may climb to the top of the tall lighthouse. The climb requires hiking up 268 steps to an open platform which surrounds the lantern at 175 feet above the sea. A breathtaking vista unfolds for those who step out on the platform.

The purpose of a lighthouse, however, is that of a sentinel to be seen by ships at sea, not as a tower to observe from. For that reason lighthouses are located along the Carolina coast, approximately 40 miles apart. Such spacing allows north and south-bound vessels to spot a light ahead before a light astern disappears.

No two lights are alike. They are different in design to help seafarers distinguish one from another. Each has its own shape, height and marking for immediate identification by day and a distinctive light that flashes at regular intervals or in unusual cadence for recognition at night.

The history of North Carolina's lighthouses includes some tumultuous events. In addition to the constant ravages of storms and the encroaching tides of the sea which wash away at their foundation, the lights have had to withstand attacks by man. They faced destructive forces of both the Confederate and Union armies during the Civil War. They

Copyright © 1982 by Jane Corey

underwent shellings by German submarines during World War I.

In recent years the U.S. Coast Guard has automated all Tar Heel lighthouses. A photo-electric eye now turns on the beacons at night and off in the morning just like street lights. The switch occurs when the level of daylight falls below or rises above a preselected point.

The lighthouse keepers who once dutifully performed the switching-on-and-off chore are almost a vanished breed. They were called "wickies" because at one time they actually fired the lanterns. Several of their homes remain beside the towers they manned. The Bodie Island and Cape Hatteras houses, for example, have been converted into museums to ensure their preservation. The dwellings remind visitors of the vigil the keepers maintained before technology rendered their services obsolete.

The "wickies" recognize that automated lights give seafarers what they ever welcome, "a beacon in the dark and an eerie blast on a foggy night." Still, the old-timers must view the changes as another strike by automation and lament that in the ways of the sea something has been lost.

INDEX TO LIGHTHOUSE EXPLORATIONS

Lighthouse	Page
1 OAK ISLAND LIGHTHOUSE	5
2 FRYING PAN LIGHT TOWER	8
3 BALDHEAD LIGHTHOUSE	12
4 PRICE'S CREEK LIGHTHOUSE	16
5 CAPE LOOKOUT LIGHTHOUSE	20
6 OCRACOKE LIGHTHOUSE	24
7 CAPE HATTERAS LIGHTHOUSE	28
8 DIAMOND SHOALS LIGHT TOWER	32
9 BODIE ISLAND LIGHTHOUSE	36
10 CURRITUCK BEACH LIGHTHOUSE	40

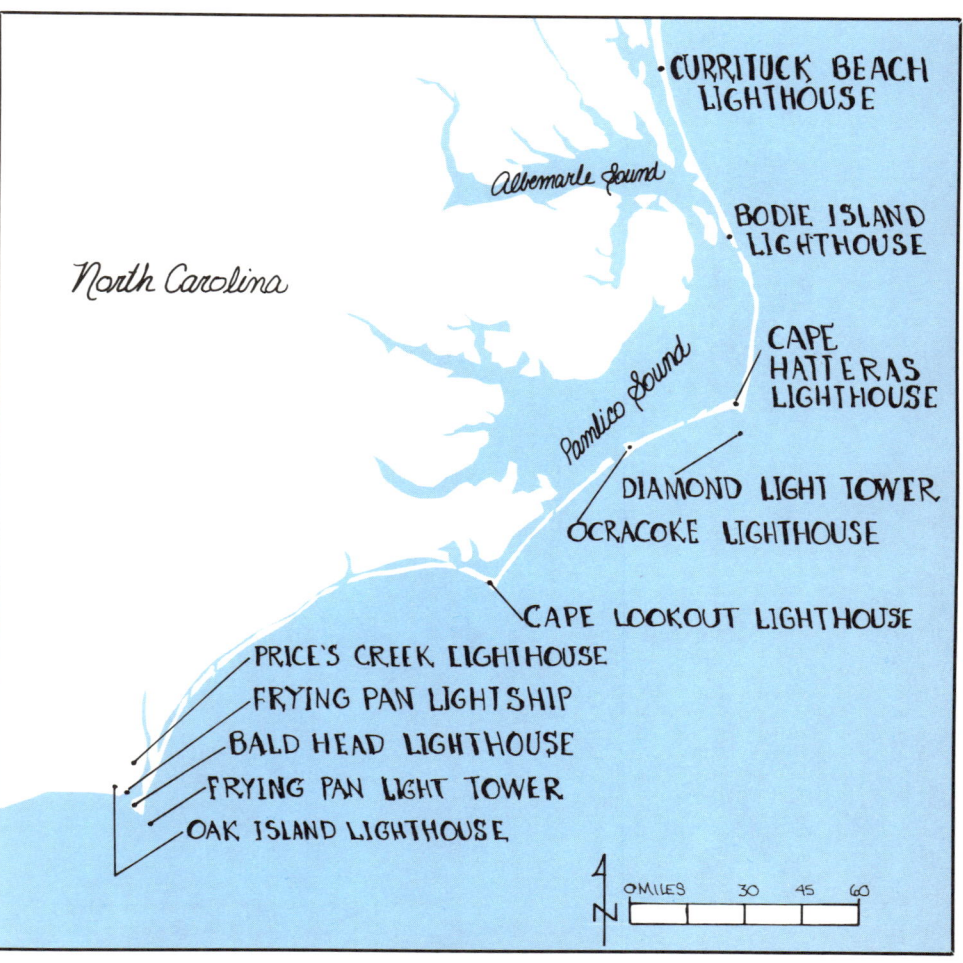

1 Oak Island Lighthouse

Oak Island Lighthouse flashes the newest and most powerful beam of all American lighthouses. The beacon began service on May 15, 1958, following placement of the lens protection assembly on top of the tower by a Marine Corps helicopter. It was the first lighthouse built on the Maryland, Virginia and North Carolina coast in 54 years.

Under normal conditions, the intensity of the light measures 1,400,000 candlepower. This strength can be increased to 20,000,000 when needed due to low visibility. In brilliancy, the beacon ranks behind only one other in the world—a French light on the English Channel.

The Oak Island signal can be seen 19 miles at sea. Four flashes go out at one-second intervals followed by six seconds of eclipse. The light generates such an intense blinding heat in the beacon room that repairmen must wear protective clothing. Even with such insulation they can work only a short time.

The U.S. Coast Guard maintains the lighthouse as part of its Oak Island Station. The complex includes a headquarters building, personnel quarters, a radar tower and boat docks. A next-door neighbor is old Fort Caswell, operated by North Carolina Baptists as a summer assembly site.

The station takes its name from Oak Island, an outer strip of North Carolina's lower southeastern coast. A bridge connects the island with the mainland below Southport.

In 1958 Oak Island Lighthouse replaced Cape Fear Lighthouse, located across the Cape Fear River on Bald Head Island. At the same time the Oak Island Station assumed operation of the radio beacon navigational aid located at "Old Baldy" Lighthouse on Bald Head Island.

The Oak Island tower rises 169 feet above water. The top third of the cylindrical structure is black, the middle third white and the lower third gray. With colors mixed in its cement covering, the tower requires no outside painting.

The lighthouse builder, W.F. Brinkley Company of

Granite Quarry, N.C., had to go 125 feet underground to reach a rock foundation solid enough to support the tower. At ground level the foundation measures 16 feet in diameter. The tower, by design, may sway as much as three feet in a 60-mile gale.

In formal ceremony on May 15, 1958, Captain Charlie Swan, an old-timer who for 55 years manned the old Cape Fear Lighthouse on Bald Head Island, threw the switch activating its successor, the Oak Island Lighthouse.

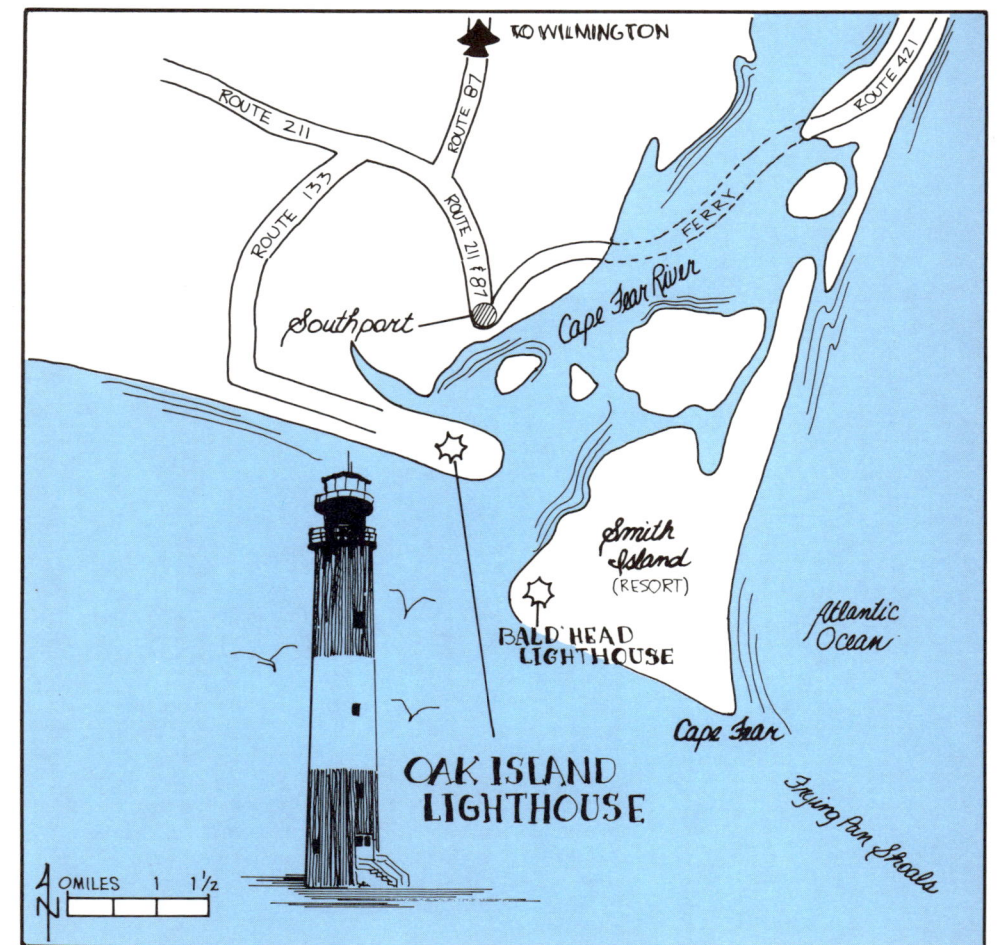

2 Frying Pan Light Tower

Frying Pan Light Tower, reaching out of the sea like a giant erector set, guides ships around the shallow waters of Frying Pan Shoals. The off-shore light supplements the on-shore warning beam of nearby Oak Island Lighthouse. Without the guidance of these two lights, vessels steering into the mouth of the Cape Fear River enroute to docks at Wilmington might easily ground on the massive reef which stretches 40 miles into the Atlantic Ocean from Southport. Its sand bars run as shallow as three or four feet in some places.

Originally, a lightship anchored off the tip of the shoals alerted passing vessels of the hazardous reef. For 110 years (1854-1964) the Frying Pan Lightship faithfully and heroically performed the duty. Apprehensive that strong hurricane winds would eventually blow the lightship from its mooring. Federal officials ordered that the vessel be replaced by a tower in 1964. The lightship (see illustration on page two) retired first to Southport as a waterfront museum piece and later in 1981 to Salisbury, Md., as part of a nautical antique shop complex.

The 125-foot-tower replacement "sways gently under pounding of the waves and twists and moans under the assault of storms" but remains firm and does the job with no personnel aboard. In 1979 a six-man crew was freed from duty on the tower when the U.S Coast Guard automated the outpost. The conversion to a computerized tower saved money and provided a system for gathering oceangraphic data.

The roof over the deckhouse, formerly the living quarters of the Coast Guardmen, serves as a helicopter deck. The deckhouse sits 40 feet above the Atlantic waters. The light itself is 125 feet above the sea.

Four giant steel columns supporting the yellow painted structure plunge 40 feet to the reef level and bore another 125 feet into the ocean bottom.

The words "Frying Pan" appear in large size on three sides of the structure.

The light consists of two 24-inch rotating beacons of 3.5 million candlepower. The beam can be seen for 17 miles at sea.

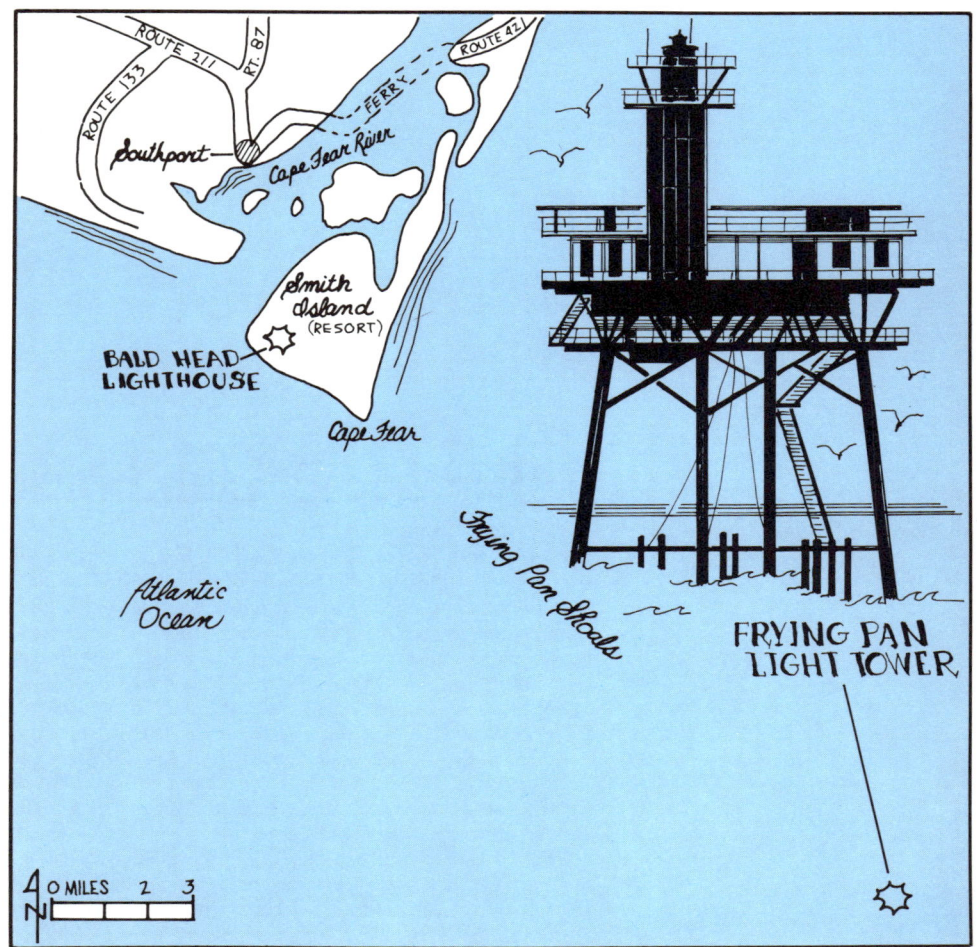

The fog signal of the tower can be heard for six miles, emitting a three-second blast every 30 seconds.

McDermott Incorporated of Harvey, La. constructed the Frying Pan Light Station. A huge barge transported the deckhouse, built in Morgan City, La., to the tower site where a super crane lifted the six-room house from the barge to the foundation of the steel tower.

Construction workers, living in Southport, flew by helicopter each day to the building site. They erected the tower to last for 75 years with maximum resistance to wind and wave action.

3 Bald Head Lighthouse

Although inoperative for years, Bald Head Lighthouse stands as the oldest lighthouse structure in North Carolina. Built in 1817, the 90-foot-high tower survives as one of three lighthouses on Bald Head Island which for 162 years guided ships into the mouth of the lower Cape Fear River near Southport. The first of the three was Bald Head Light (1796). It was torn down to build the second Bald Head Lighthouse (1817). The third Cape Fear Lighthouse (1903) operated until it was demolished and replaced in 1958 by a new lighthouse on nearby Oak Island. The 1817 Bald Head Lighthouse alone stands among the three towers which once cast beams from Bald Head Island.

"Bald Head Island" is actually a colloquial name for a large island and a surrounding group of smaller islands known collectively as Smith Island. The most prominent feature of the large island, a round sand dune near the river side of its southernmost ridge, resembles the bald head of a man. The island complex and the lighthouse take their name from this landmark.

The abandoned tower stands as the focal point of the island's semitropical setting. A rich forest contains huge live oaks, palms, tall palmettoes, cedars, hollies and loblolly pines. Abundant wildlife includes cranes, ospreys and Loggerhead turtles.

Unspoiled sandy beaches and numerous freshwater lagoons rim the 3½-mile-wide island. At the lower end of the ocean side is the point called Cape Fear. Extending offshore from it are the dangerous Frying Pan Shoals. Pelicans and other birds roost on the exposed "lumps" of the shoals.

In the 1960s and 70s the question of preserving Bald Head Island in its natural state was the subject of heated debate between conservationists and land developers. A

compromise eventually provided that parts of the island may be developed and other parts are to remain natural. With this opening to limited development an exclusive resort featuring an 18-hole golf course began taking form in 1970. "Old Baldy," as one writer affectionately described the lighthouse, has been carefully preserved by the resort owners as a symbol and landmark that can easily be sighted from practically all angles of the island.

A rewarding vista of the "paradise" island awaits those who climb to the top of the old lighthouse (112 wooden steps). The sea appears off one side of the island and the Cape Fear River, Southport and the distant mainland appear off the other.

A metallic frame of nine rusty bars, which once held glass to protect the light, extends from the top of the tower. The frame sits just off-center. During its early years the lighthouse burned whale oil in the lantern and emitted a beam 110 feet above the sea at high water. The light was visible for 18 miles.

In 1816 Congress appropriated $16,000 to build Old Baldy. The authorization specified that the lighthouse be built of hard brick, octagonal in shape, 90 feet in height and rough plastered on the outside. It was also to be constructed about a mile up shore from the 1796 lighthouse; bricks from it were to be used. Daniel S. Way won the construction contract as low bidder.

In 1866 the Federal Government extinguished Old Baldy following erection of a new light at the nearby New Inlet entrance. Four years later, Old Baldy was relit when the new light became useless as a result of the closing of the New Inlet channel following construction of "The Rocks" seawall.

Old Baldy's come-back was short-lived. Because it lay so far inland and inadequately warned sea captains of the hazardous Frying Pan Shoals, the lighthouse was replaced in 1903 by the 150-foot-high Cape Fear Lighthouse on the southern tip of Bald Head Island.

Old Baldy became a fourth-order fixed light and remained in this capacity until 1935. It was relegated in 1941 to the function of a radio beacon for the U.S. Navy, which at that time used Fort Caswell across the mouth of the Cape Fear River and needed such a beacon. The radio beacon directed ships into the river channel in thick weather when the Cape Fear Lighthouse beam was obscured. Old Baldy discontinued as a radio beacon in 1958 when the new Oak Island Lighthouse Station assumed that responsibility. Old Baldy had become obsolete.

Still, the old-timer continues to stand, defying the toll of weather and time. Conveniently reached by boat from Southport, it survives proudly as a romantic vestige of Tar Heel maritime history.

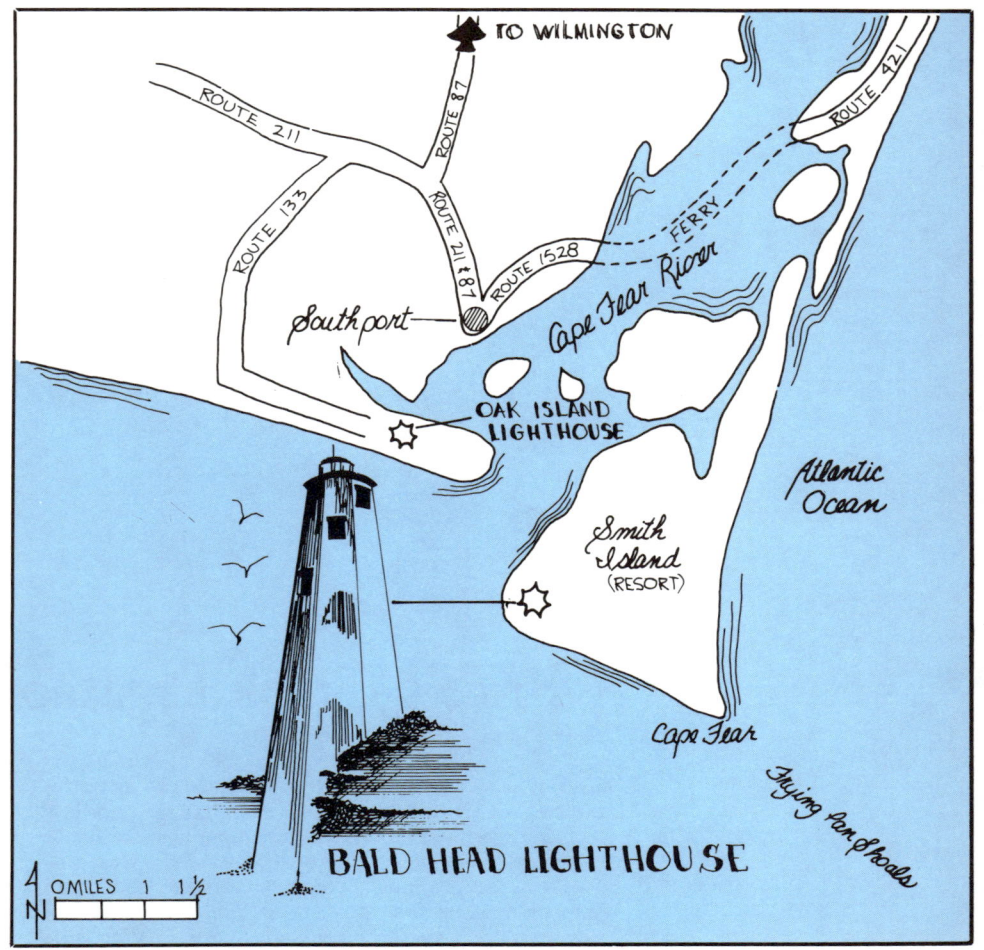

4 Price's Creek Lighthouse

Price's Creek Lighthouse remains as the only vestige of a chain of lights built during 1848-51 to guide an increasing traffic of vessels along the 25-mile stretch of the Cape Fear River from its mouth to Wilmington. Long abandoned, the lighthouse tower sits on the west bank of the river near Price's Creek, about two miles above Southport. Permission is needed to visit the site, located on the property of a chemical company. The tower, however, may be seen from the state ferry which crosses the Cape Fear between Southport and Fort Fisher.

Other links in the original series of lights along the Cape Fear included beacons at the "upper jetty," Campbell's Island, Orton's Point, Oak Island and the "Horse Shoe" between New Inlet and Price's Creek. All became obsolete and have long since vanished except the deteriorated tower of Price's Creek Lighthouse and the foundation of the Campbell Island Lighthouse.

In 1848 the U.S. Congress appropriated funds for the erection of these beacons. The appropriation for Price's Creek Lighthouse and another tower totaled $6,000. The construction contract specified dimensions of 20 feet in height and 17 feet in diameter at the base and 9 feet at the top. It was to be built of hard brick in a round shape with an iron lantern top containing six lights. The keeper's home was to face the back beacon of the tower.

During the War Between the States, Price's Creek Lighthouse served as a Confederate signal station; it was the only means of communication across the Cape Fear River.

According to James Sprunt's *Tales and Traditions of the Lower Cape Fear*, "the Confederate States Signal Corps frequently rendered efficient service to the blockade runners after they had succeeded in getting between the blockaders and the beach, where they were in danger of the shore batteries until their character became known to the forts."

Confederate forces retained control of the Cape Fear River until the second battle of Fort Fisher in January 1865. Before surrendering to the Union, the Southern defenders destroyed or made inoperative most of the lights in the Cape Fear area including the small Price's Creek Lighthouse.

After the Civil War, in 1867, the U.S. Light List showed Price's Creek Lighthouse as "not re-established."

The top of the abandoned Price's Creek Lighthouse as rendered in the map illustration differs from the watercolor version. The latter is the most current view.

19

5 Cape Lookout Lighthouse

In 1873 a U.S. Light Service crew painted a black and white diamond pattern on the Cape Lookout Lighthouse to enhance its value as a day mark. Reportedly, the painters put on the wrong pattern. Some students of American lighthouses say the diamond design should have been placed on the lighthouse at Cape Hatteras which overlooks Diamond Shoals and the candy striped pattern on the Hatteras tower should have been applied on the Cape Lookout tower. David Stick, noted Outer Banks historian, writes* that this oft-repeated story is an erroneous one. The painters correctly followed their instructions and did not make a mistake, Stick maintains.

Error or not, it makes little difference which lighthouse bears the diamond design. It might be argued that the diamond marking probably would have been more appropriate on the Cape Hatteras light since the reef it overlooks is diamond-like in shape and bears the name Diamond Shoals. Yet the alternate black and white lozenges appear quite handsome on the Cape Lookout tower.

The Cape Lookout light was constructed in 1859. It replaced a structure erected in 1812, which was difficult to see at dusk and dawn because of the "mist which rises above the horizon between the vessel and the lamp." The new 160-foot structure, with a fixed white light of 160,000 candlepower, corrected the problem and has since clearly marked the important headland south of Cape Hatteras and guided mariners around the treacherous 10-mile-long Lookout Shoals. Early maps show the light's location on the outer point of Core Banks as "Promontorium tremendum," translated by sailors to mean "Horrible Headland."

Storm and tide years ago drove a settlement of inhabitants on Cape Lookout to more sheltered Shackleford Banks. That 19th century lost community, once a whaling industry, was known as Diamond City, its name probably prompted by the lighthouse marking. At the site human skeletons have been uncovered by shifting sands.

The Cape Lookout Lighthouse is reached by boat from nearby Harkers Island or from the towns of Beaufort and

---

* *The Lighthouses of North Carolina* by David Stick, 1980 (North Carolina Department of Archives and History, Raleigh, N.C.)

Morehead City. On the ride across the sound visitors see porpoises cartwheeling in waves and wild ponies galloping on marshs of adjacent Shackleford Banks.

A pile of rubble is about all that remains of the prior lighthouse on Cape Lookout. Authorized by Congress in 1804, it began service sometime in 1812 and was painted with red and white horizontal stripes in 1845. Drifting sand soon threatened the base of that structure and officials decided in 1857 to build the present tower. Since then time and the elements have reduced the old structure to a pile of rubble barely recognizable.

The present light, lit on November 1, 1859, became a model for all lighthouses subsequently constructed on the Outer Banks. A Confederate raiding force ruined its lens in 1861. Refitted, the light reappeared in 1863 only to be damaged again in 1865 when Confederate raiders dynamited the tower, destroying the lower stairs. The following year Congress appropriated funds to replace the wooden stairs with iron ones.

In 1873 the U.S. Lighthouse Board assigned Cape Lookout Lighthouse its present diamond-shape marking. Because neighboring lighthouses appeared almost identical, the Board decreed that each bear a distinct marking. Cape Lookout would be checkered, Cape Hatteras would have spiral bands, Bodie Island would have horizontal bands, and Currituck would retain its natural red brick appearance with no marking.

In 1914 the fixed white beacon of the Cape Lookout Lighthouse was changed to the present double flash. Five shipwrecks occurred during the three-year period prior to the change and none afterward during a similar period.

In 1950 Cape Lookout became an unwatched light. Man gave way to an electronic device in controlling the illumination of the region through the 160,000-candlepower beacon.

In 1979 the National Park Service, owner of the historic lighthouse (the U.S. Coast Guard operates it), condemned

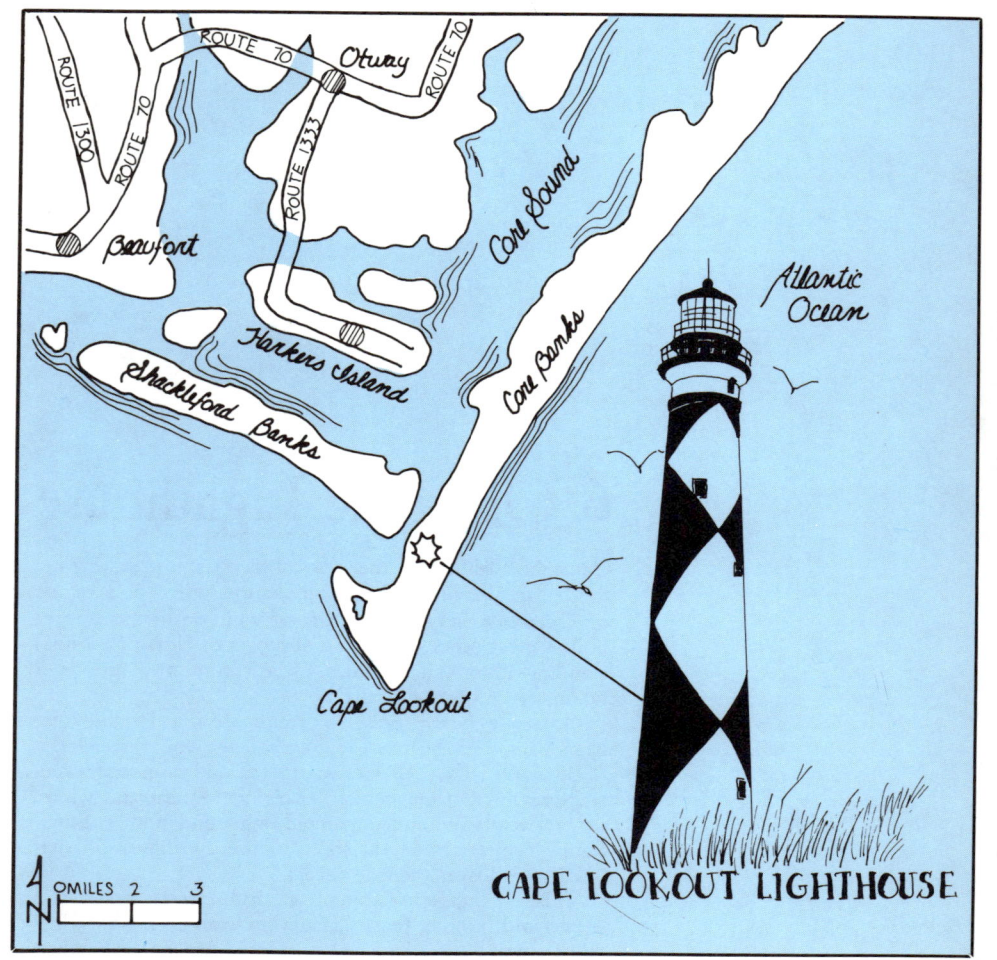

the tower to fall victim to tides and other forces of the sea from which the light had served as protection so long. The sea had steadily nibbled away the shoreline around the lighthouse. Surveys showed almost 1,000 feet of land between the lighthouse and the sound had crumpled away between 1940 and 1979. The most severe erosion occurred during 1977-78 when 120 feet of land washed away. Some observers predicted the remaining 250 feet between the shore and lighthouse would vanish within a short period of time.

Many parties want to preserve the historic lighthouse but none has identified money for the expensive undertaking. Questions, therefore, remain: Will preservationists find resources to save the tower? Will the structure eventually succumb to the onslought of weather and sea?

6 Ocracoke Lighthouse

Ocracoke Lighthouse, the oldest beacon still operating on the North Carolina coast, overlooks the little fishing village of Ocracoke. Its conical shaft of whitewashed masonry, unlike most other lighthouse outposts of North Carolina, stands within the confines of a community and is a landmark of that settlement.

Ocracoke is the only community on a 16-mile-long island, also called Ocracoke. Sandy lanes wind through the 500-person village. Cedar, wax-myrtle and yaupon thickets stabilize the shifting sands. Fences, some neat and white, others weathered and unpainted, surround homes. Small family cemeteries adjoin some of the dwellings. Gnarled oaks spread over the tiny yards.

Villagers engage in fishing (e.g., drum, trout, mullet, and blues) and hunting (e.g., Canada geese and pintails). They work out of Silver Lake harbor, which opens to the Pamlico Sound and the ocean via a channel called the "Ditch." Small dinghies bob on the lake water and larger vessels tie up at docks. Ferries connect the island with the mainland. The Ocracoke Lighthouse, quaint and charming, guides the "coming and going" of the vessels.

In 1823, builders made the lighthouse a handsome as well as functional navigational aid. During the busy 1840s the sentinel in its traditional, simple form gave day and night bearings to a monthly average of more than 100 oceangoing sailing vessels entering the Ocracoke Inlet.

Since the 76-foot-high tower was first lighted, keepers have painted it white In the early days they used a whitewash concocted by the U.S. Lighthouse Board. The Board's recipe for a batch called for such ingredients as half a bushel of unslaked lime with boiling water, a peck of salt, half a pound of powdered Spanish whiting, three pounds of

ground rice put in boiling water and a pound of clear glue. Painters applied the mix hot as possible to the structure.

In 1822 the U.S. Congress approved and appropriated funds for construction of the present Ocracoke Lighthouse. Such authorization earlier came from the North Carolina Legislature but the state relinquished its authority in 1789 when the Federal government assumed as a national obligation the responsibility for lighthouse construction and maintenance along the coasts of the country.

The new Ocracoke light replaced two former ones which proved ineffective. The first, a 54-foot wooden tower completed in 1798, stood on Shell Castle Island just inside the entrance to Ocracoke Inlet where the pirate Blackbeard (Edward Teach) once lived. Because of a change in the channel, the light tower became useless and was replaced in 1820 by a light vessel in the inlet. Within two years shifting sands rendered the vessel also valueless and in 1822 Congress authorized $20,000 to construct the present lighthouse. It is the oldest active light on the North Carolina coast.

Built by Noah Porter of Massachusetts on a two-acre site bought from Jacob Gaskill, the tower measures 65 feet from the ground to the center of the lantern. At first the keeper's house with a gable roof was a one-story dwelling; later a second story was added. A shed, once the storage for whale oil, still stands beside the lighthouse base. A white picket fence encircles the entire complex.

During the early stage of the War between the States, the lens of the Ocracoke Lighthouse was removed but in 1863 was refitted and put back into service. In 1868 the tower was cemented and covered with two coats of whitewash. Inspectors gave it a rating of "fine" order.

Whale oil originally served as fuel to light the lanterns behind the reflecting lens. Later, kerosene replaced the whale oil and finally electrical power controlled by automated devices replaced it. Now equipped with a fourth-order lamp, the lighthouse projects an 8,000-candlepower fixed white light visible for 14 miles. Like a street light, it automatically turns on at night and off in the morning.

Light beacon technology has kept the Ocracoke Lighthouse useful over the years even though the sand and currents around the island have shifted considerably. Despite all the technical advancement in warning ships of dangers, many through the years have gone down off the island.

7 Cape Hatteras Lighthouse

Cape Hatteras Lighthouse towers 208 feet—the tallest in America. The light warns seafarers of treacherous waters off the Cape, seas so hazardous that the area is known as the "Graveyard of the Atlantic" because of its legacy of ships in distress and shipwrecks. Hundreds have foundered there.

The shallow Diamond Shoals and two strong ocean currents make the zone dangerous. The shoals, barely submerged sandbars, jut about 14 miles into the Atlantic from the Cape. The two currents, a cold southbound Artic one and a warm northbound Gulfstream one, flow close to the shoals. Ships taking advantage of these currents as shipping lanes must follow a narrow channel or run aground on the shoals. Compounding the vessels' difficulty are turbulent waters where the cold and warm currents collide, bad weather and poor navigation. There is also the problem of recognizing at sea landmarks along the low sand dunes of the Cape through a blanket of haze which frequently forms over the shoals.

To make it easier to be seen from the sea the Cape Hatteras Lighthouse was built as America's tallest, a vigil recognizable day and night for a distance of 20 miles. To supplement the onshore lighthouse as a navigational aid in guiding ships by the Diamond Shoals, the Federal government in 1824 began anchoring at one time or another a lightship 14 miles offshore at the end of the shoals. In 1966 the lightship was replaced by a permanent offshore "Texas" light tower (see page 32 on Diamond Shoals Light Tower).

The present Cape Hatteras Lighthouse stands as the second of three lights that have shone from the elbow bend of Cape Hatteras. In 1794 Congress authorized the first light, following persistent complaints about the dangerous Carolina coast. Completed about 10 years later, it began operation with problems. The dim light on the tower, for example, could not effectively ensure a safe coast and natives criticized the tower as "an eye sore and a disgrace to the Hatteras community." In 1861 shells from a Federal fleet damaged the light, further marring its appearance.

In response to these problems, Congress appropriated money for a new Cape Hatteras Lighthouse, the present structure. It was erected in 1869-70 by the U.S. Lighthouse Board (later the Lighthouse Service, now part of the U.S. Coast Guard). The tall tower extends 225 feet above sea level. It rests on layers of pine timbers, submerged below the low tide level to prevent rotting. An examination of the

foundation in 1947 disclosed no deterioration of the then 78-year-old timbers.

The walls of the tower measure 13 feet thick at the base. They contain 1,200,000 bricks manufactured at a kiln on the James River near Richmond, Virginia. A Vermont quarry supplied the support stone.

These and other construction materials were brought in through the sound, unloaded on a wharf extending into the sound and transported over a tram railway from the end of the wharf to the lighthouse construction site.

Cement wash covers the fabric of the tower to protect it against weathering. In 1873 workmen painted the tower's distinctive day marking of four spirals—two black and two white. Each spiral revolves around the structure 1½ times. The stripes give it a giant candy cane appearance.

Light, intensified through a first-order Fresnel lens, first flashed from the present tower on December 16, 1870.

The lighthouse, ironically, has never been free from constant torment of the sea from which it was built to protect man and ship. When constructed, it was positioned more than ½ mile from the sea. By 1919 tides rolled within 300 feet. By 1935 waves reached its base and the Federal Government abandoned the lighthouse. In 1936, a third tower, a steel skeleton structure, was established temporarily about two miles northeast in Buxton Woods.

To buttress the abandoned lighthouse from the sea, erosion fighters drove sheet steel piling into the sand around its base. The Civilian Conservation Corps (CCC) erected sand fences on the beach and planted grass and sea oats on man-made dunes. Those efforts and probably some changes in natural tendencies halted the shore erosion and officials judged the position of the lighthouse safe again from the sea. On January 23, 1950 the light from the temporary skeleton tower was transferred back to the long-standing brick lighthouse and the old-timer was reactivated.

The Cape Hatteras Lighthouse retained its superlative status as the tallest in America. Other lights in the nation are at higher elevation above sea level but only because they rest on bluffs and promontories. Officials responsible for the upkeep and preservation of the Cape Hatteras structure undoubtedly wish it rested on higher ground. They must maintain a constant eye on the approaching sea, which slowly nibbles away the narrow beach between the tower and the water.

In 1981 state leaders launched a fund-raising campaign to protect the lighthouse from the sea.

Fresnel lenses built by Henry le Paute of Paris were used in the first lighthouse and the present one at Hatteras. They intensified the small oilwick flame at the top of the tower into a powerful light of considerable strength. In 1861 a retreating Confederate force carried away the original lamp used in the first lighthouse. It was never found. When the present brick tower was temporarily abandoned in 1935, vandals badly damaged the lens, which was replaced by a rotating beacon when the light was reactivated in 1950.

The 36-inch duplex rotating beacon, with one 1,000-watt lamp in each beacon, produces a beam of 250,000-candle power normally visible for about 20 miles. The beam, however, has been observed at sea at a distance of 51 miles and in the air at a distance of 115 miles.

A master clock of Swiss design, known as an astronomic time switch, controls the light. The clock is adjusted to turn the light on 30 minutes before sunset and off 30 minutes after sunrise. The light shines 191 feet above mean high water. To reach it one must climb 268 steps inside the tower. The U.S. Coast Guard owns and operates the lighting equipment.

The National Park Service acquired ownership of the Cape Hatteras Lighthouse itself when the Coast Guard abandoned the tower in 1935. Now part of the Cape Hatteras National Seashore, it is opened to the public. Adjacent to the tower is the former lightkeeper's house. It has been converted into a "Museum of the Sea," an interesting visitor attraction.

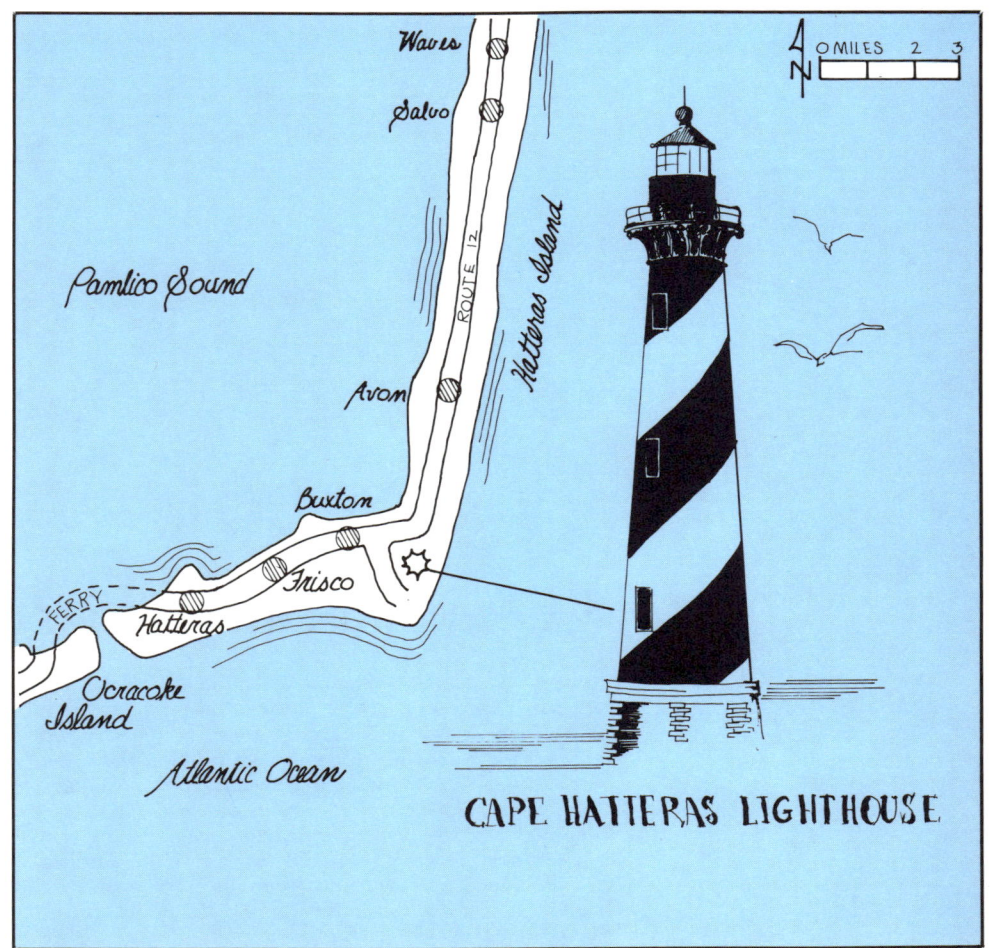

8 Diamond Shoals Light Tower

Diamond Shoals Light Station sticks out of the Atlantic Ocean on four great steel legs. Thirteen miles offshore from Cape Hatteras, the 175-foot-high tower warns ships of shallow sand bars which if unavoided would wreck them. Northbound and southbound currents collide to form shoals in a diamond-shaped area, hence the name Diamond Shoals. During the past 400 years hundreds of ships have fallen victim to the sea along this segment of the Carolina coast. Bits and pieces of victims, long submerged in sand and surf, occasionally surface as reminders of the "Graveyard of the Atlantic."

The Diamond tower is one of seven offshore light stations along the East Coast. Eventually all will be automated. Stations at Savannah, Ga. and Brenton Reef, R.I. and Diamond were the first to undergo the transition.

The Diamond tower was erected in 1966. It replaced lightships anchored in the waters off Cape Hatteras during much of the time since 1824. In that year a lightship first moored at the end of the shoals to supplement the warning beacon of nearby Cape Hatteras Lighthouse. It wasn't until 1897 that mooring techniques improved to the extent that a

lightship became a permanent fixture on the shoals. Several successors were rammed by passing ships and in 1918 the Diamond Shoals lightship was sunk by a German submarine. It was succeeded by another lightship. In 1966 that vessel, following activation of the off-shore Diamond tower, was reassigned to the Massachusetts coast and renamed the Boston Lightship.

Coast Guard men usually reach the Diamond Shoals Light Station by boat. It is also accessible by helicopter; a sturdy "whirly bird" pad tops the structure.

Three navigational aids on the Diamond light tower help vessels steer clear of the surrounding treacherous waters. They are a powerful light that can be seen up to 20 miles from the tower, a foghorn and a radio beacon that broadcasts the initials "DS, DS, DS" in continuous Morse Code.

Electronic equipment controls the navigational aids. The tower, identified in large letters on all four sides simply as "Diamond," is completely automated. Should a light bulb, generator or any other critical equipment fail, backup units immediately replace them and an automatic radio signal summons a repair crew from the mainland.

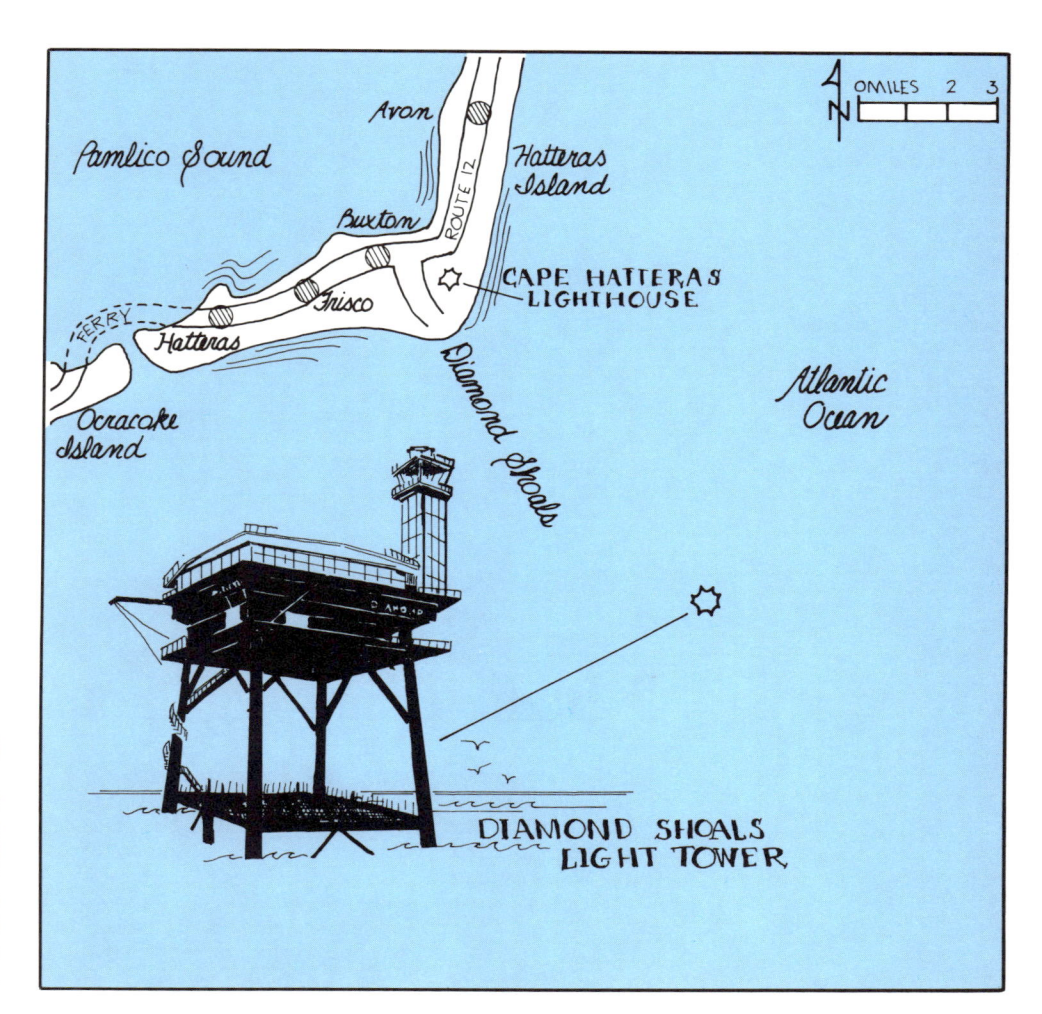

    The U.S. Coast Guard is responsible for maintaining the "Texas" tower, so-called because of its similarity to the elevated, stilt-legged towers used in Texas for offshore oil drilling. The Coast Guard automated the operation in 1977 and transferred the six-man crew that tended the light to other stations. The change-over marked the first time in 153 years that Atlantic mariners relied entirely on machines, not men, to warn them of the dangers of the Diamond Shoals.

9 Bodie Island Lighthouse

Lighthouses along the North Carolina coast suffered heavy damage during the Civil War. As navigational aids, they largely benefited Northern ships since the Union Navy held sea superiority. The "Yankees," taking full advantage of their naval strength, shelled Confederate defenses, blockaded Southern shipping routes and occupied coastal land. The Confederacy, determined that the lighthouses would not be taken intact as Federal aids, swiftly damaged the beacons along the Carolina coast whenever such damage served the Southern cause. Eventually troops in gray put all lights out of commission. In January 1865, following defeat in a battle at Fort Fisher, the Confederates extinguished in the Cape Fear River area the last lights under their control.

The present Bodie Island Lighthouse (pronounced "body") replaced a structure completely demolished in 1862 by Confederate troops. A "rebel" band infiltrated the Union-held Outer Banks and blew up the lighthouse. The

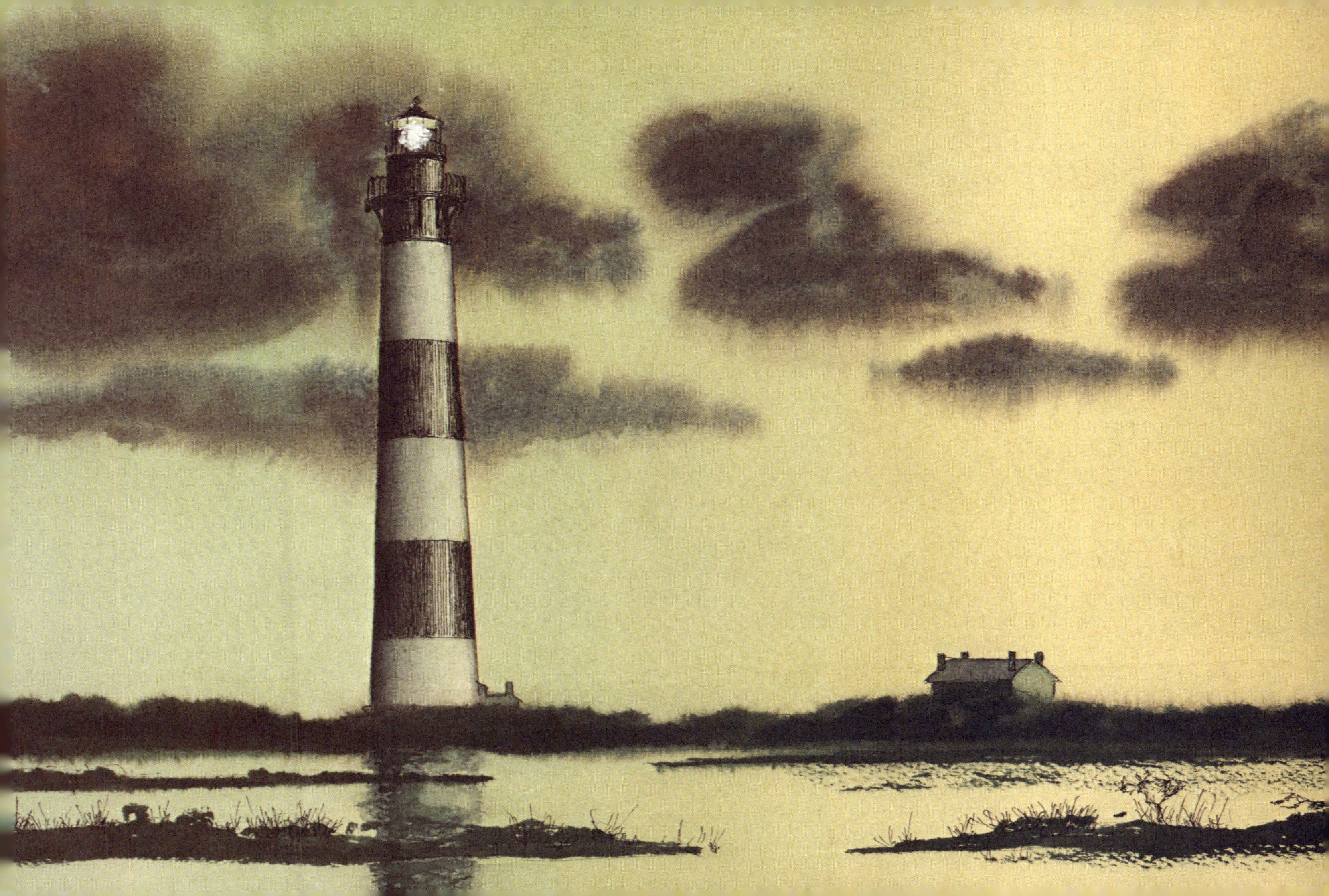

destroyed light had just been rebuilt in 1859 as an improvement to the original beacon constructed in 1847.

The present tower, the third one, stands north of Oregon Inlet on a site bought for $150 from John B. Etheridge. The 150-foot-high structure, costing $140,000, was lit on October 1, 1872.

Shortly thereafter, according to the keeper, "a flock of wild geese flew against the lantern breaking three panes of glass and considerably damaging the lens apparatus."

Repairs were made quickly, including the placement of a wire screen around the lantern as protection against future bird hits.

Tall and slim, the tower bears day markings of broad alternate black and white circular bands. It throws a 160,000-candlepower beam visible for 19 miles.

The old keeper's quarters has been converted into a visitors' center and natural history museum by managers of the Cape Hatteras National Seashore. The first national seashore recreational area (established in 1953) includes the southern part of Bodie Island.

Visitors to the Bodie Island Lighthouse may participate in 25 or more activities offered by the National Park Service. These include sitting on the back porch and chatting with an old keeper about the light, hearing a recitation on the history of shipwrecks and lifesaving on the Outer Banks, stalking birds with a park naturalist, wading in marshes for a firsthand look at plants and animals and bathing at nearby Coquina Beach, named for the shellfish of the conch family.

10 Currituck Beach Lighthouse

In 1875 the new Currituck Beach Lighthouse lit the one remaining dark spot on the Atlantic coast of North America: a 40-mile gap between Virginia's Cape Henry Lighthouse and North Carolina's Bodie Island Lighthouse. Each of the two lights, 80 miles apart, could be seen for a distance of 19 miles. The 40 miles in the middle where no light was visible either north or south left a dangerous blind stretch. Many southbound ships sailed close inshore along the stretch to avoid the north-flowing current of the Gulf Stream. The dark area took a heavy toll of ships and lives.

To end this problem, Currituck Beach Lighthouse was built in 1874-75 on Whalehead Hill halfway between Cape Henry and Bodie Island on land bought from Edmund C.

41

Lindsey. Its first-order lens threw a flashing beam 19 miles in either direction.

The red brick tower, constructed at a cost of $178,000, stands 158 feet above sea level. It is supported underground on piles with heavy timber cribbing for foundation on the sandy terrain.

The lighthouse entrance, larger and more charming than entrances of other towers, served for years as a workshop. It also housed storage tanks for oil that had to be carried up the 150-foot-high steel staircase. The steel staircase not only reduced the risk of fire in the interior of the tower but strengthened the building. The steps at the base divide around a cistern built within the tower.

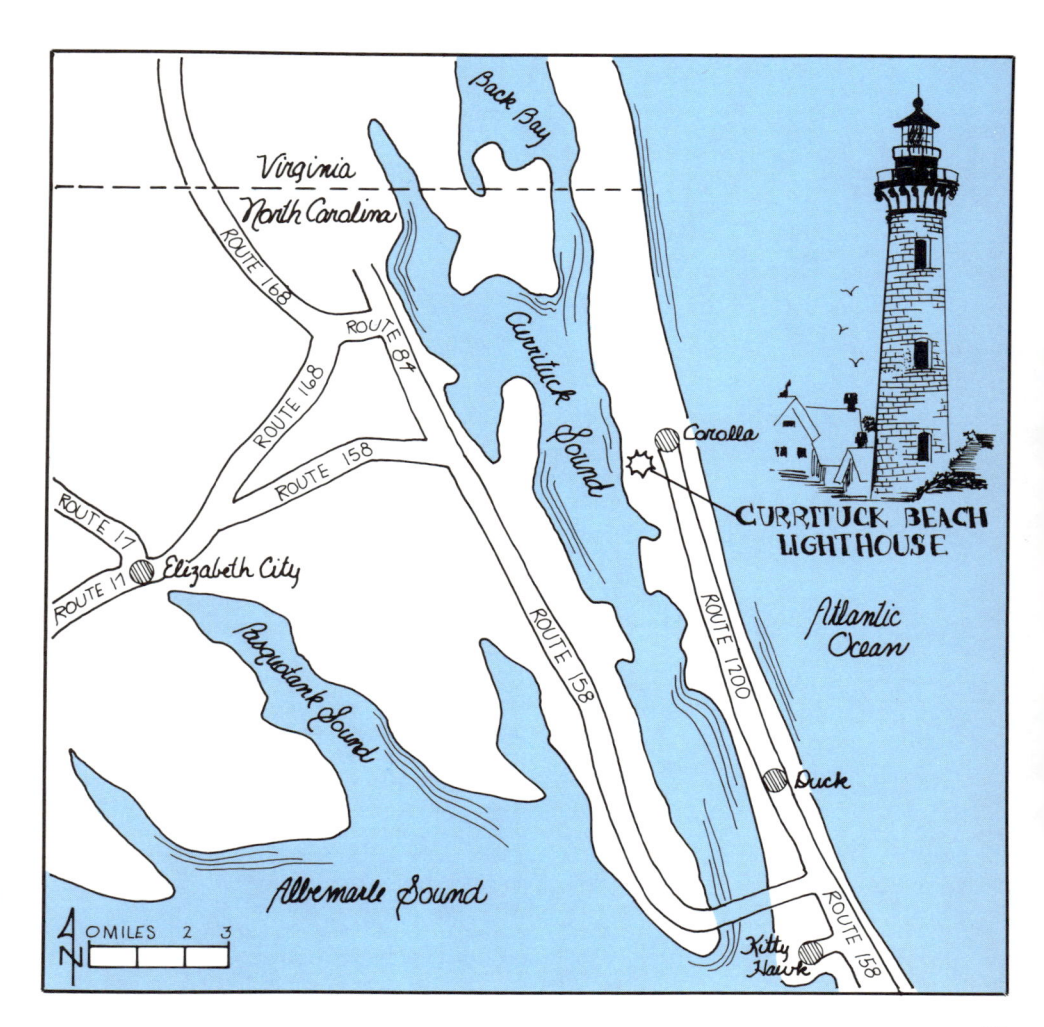

The unpainted lighthouse, often called Whalehead, stands at the village of Corolla, south of the Virginia line and north of Kitty Hawk.

Its 160,000-candlepower beacon is electronically controlled.

About the Author and Artists

CINDY COREY visited her first North Carolina lighthouse as a little girl. On a cold December night she and her father pitched camp at the foot of the Cape Hatteras Lighthouse but soon withdrew to a nearby motel to escape a hard winter rain.

Years later, while sitting in the historic preservation class of Professor J. Edwin Hendricks at Wake Forest University, Miss Corey recalled the chilly trip to the sentinel on the Outer Banks and decided to explore one day all the Tar Heel lighthouses. She had learned that the days of the aging beacons are numbered. The sea is eroding away some of their foundations and the need for them is now minimal since most modern vessels are equipped with navigational devices. In a word, lighthouses are becoming obsolete.

The Carolinian wanted to inspect the historic Tar Heel assets, report on their condition and in a sense romanticize them. She thought a publication describing and illustrating their beauty and history and pinpointing their sites would increase interest in their preservation.

This is that book.

Cindy Corey trekked to the Carolina lighthouses generally in company of friends and family. Like her mother and sister, both of whom write about North Carolina, she possesses a keen interest in her home state. Keeping a tab on its finer things are a tradition and hobby of the family.

Miss Corey knows her Carolina corners. Born in Boone, she has resided at several locations across the state and traveled widely among its towns and cities as a photographer, tournament tennis player and researcher. Her home darkroom spills over with photographs of Tar Heel scenes snapped with her 35mm Nikon camera. Her closets bulge with tennis trophies, including two for the North Carolina womens' doubles championship and singles finalist in 1980. Her current research is on the old mills and great estates of North Carolina.

A graduate of Wake Forest University, she is employed by the Xerox Corporation.

KEITH ROSE specializes in watercolor seascapes. Although the former chemical businessman occasionally does other subjects, he is best known for coastal scenes. The ocean and the shore are his love and he conveys a special feeling for them. The Greensboro artist captures, according to one critic, "the rustic beauty of fishing villages, the fun of the beaches, the action of marsh—and the many other faces and moods of the North Carolina coast."

Rose's works grace the walls of financial institutions, corporate headquarters, art galleries and universities from Wilmington to Asheville. They are part of numerous personal collections from Connecticut to Florida and have appeared in many one-man shows.

It was at an exhibition of Rose's paintings in the Morehead Planetarium at Chapel Hill that the Provincial Press first saw his work and commissioned Rose to illustrate the lighthouses of North Carolina. How well the artist responded is reflected in the ten full-page watercolors in the book.

Keith Rose was born in 1920 in Washington, D.C. He attended college at Virginia Military Institute, expecting to follow his father in a military career. He went to work in the chemical industry, however, and pursued a 30-year career in research and development. His interest in art began early in this period and with study and practice it grew until it became obsessional, leading Rose to abandon chemistry in 1975 and make art a full-time occupation. That move was followed by a steady increase in sales, the winning of purchase and prize awards and the teaching of art in workshops and classes in his studio.

Rose has served as an officer in several regional art leagues and as president of the Watercolor Society of North Carolina. An avid tennis player and booster of the game, he painted a 14- by 4-foot mural of the world's top tennis stars in Greensboro's Spencer Love Tennis Center.

KATE RUSSELL FORBES drew the maps in this volume. It is her third North Carolina publication, the others being EXPLORING THE COUNTRY INNS OF NORTH CAROLINA and EXPLORING THE VILLAGES OF NORTH CAROLINA.

Mrs. Forbes also created a series of four silkscreens called the "North Carolina Suite." The beautiful prints form an imaginary landscape representing a cross-section of the state—the mountains, piedmont, coastal plains and seacoast.

The talented artist, however, works primarily in woodcuts and tapestry with drawings of Victorian Houses a favorite sideline. She has taught art for several years and exhibited in many private and public showings.

Born and raised in Atlanta, Mrs. Forbes was graduated from Stephens College in Columbia, Mo. (associate degree) and the University of North Carolina at Chapel Hill (bachelor's degree in studio art). She has lived in Frankfurt (Germany), Richmond and Asheville.

A mother of two children, she resides with her family in Salem, Virginia.

Acknowledgements

I thank all members of my family, particularly my mother and father, for all their contributions. I also extend appreciation to the many others who verified, corrected and suggested information. Especial acknowledgement is extended to J. Edwin Hendricks, professor of history, Wake Forest University; John Husted, retired engineer, Tehachapi, California; Carolyn Husted, teacher, Trona, California; R.L. Scheina, historian, United States Coast Guard, Washington, D.C.; and David Stick, Outer Banks author and historian, Kitty Hawk.

Cindy Corey

Raleigh, North Carolina